# अनमोल

Collection of hindi and english poems

P. JAYASHREE

First Published in December 2021

**ISBN: 978-93-5472-905-8**


**BLUEROSE PUBLISHERS**
www.bluerosepublishers.com
info@bluerosepublishers.com
+91 8882 898 898

**Cover Design:**
Geetika

**Typographic Design:**
Namrata Saini

**Distributed by:** BlueRose, Amazon, Flipkart, Shopclues

# सांसें

ऐ ज़िन्दगी
तुझमें क्या खूबी है
हमने तो चाहा तुझे
तू छोड़ चली
संग चलूँ या रुक जाऊँ
इसी सोच में थी
ज़िन्दगी निकल पड़ी
छोड़ मुझे अकेली
ज़िन्दगी को ज़िन्दगी से
बिछड़े मुद्दतें हो गयी
पर न कोई गिला या शिकवा
ठहरी हुई ज़िन्दगी
जीती हूँ
सांसें लेने को भी
जीना कहते हैं ना

I am busy
But not in a way all of you think
I was busy, taking deeper breath
I was busy, silencing my thoughts
I was busy, impending my emotions
I was busy, straightening my mind
I was busy, suppressing my feelings
I was busy, hiding my pains
I was busy. Capturing my tears
I was busy, trashing my heart
I was busy, searching myself
I was busy, like everyone else
Not in a way all of you think

# उड़ा लेती है

उड़ा लेती है
कुछ ना कुछ
तेरी हँसी देखकर
मुस्कुराहट उड़ गई
तेरा चेहरा देखकर
दर्द उड़ गया
तेरी आवाज़ सुनकर
होश उड़ गई
तेरे साथ बैठकर
भूख उड़ गई
तेरी याद आई
नींद उड़ गई
तू मिलने आया तो
मैं उड़ गई

Words
My way of expressing
Myself
My way of living
my dreams
My way of showing
my love
My way of spending
my life
My way of showing
My gratitude to you
My way of thanking almighty
For all I got
My way of fulfilling
My souls wish
Words......

# एक पल

एक पल शुरू
एक पल ख़त्म
पल में मिलना
पल में बिछुड़ना

इन पलों के दरमियान
कुछ लम्हे, कुछ यादें
बेशुमार दर्द दिल के
कुछ आँसू न दिखने वाले

वो पल भी था,
जब हम मुस्कुराते थे
कभी उनकी खुशी में
तो कभी वो हमारी खुशी में
अभी वो पास नहीं
वो पुराने एहसास नहीं
वो यादों का पल
हँसी को नमी बनाती है
उनकी कमी रुलाती है
एक वो पल था
एक ये पल है

# आशियाना

मैंने रेत का आशियाना बनाया
बारिश को खबर कर दिया

पंखों से ख्वाब सजाया
हवा को खबर कर दिया

पानी से तकदीर लिखा
धूप को खबर कर दिया

खुद को खुद से चुराना चाहा
फ़ना होकर खबर फैला दिया

At times I tend to
Extend my endurance
To see where it leads
Disturbing the idiocy of life
Taking an indulgent movement
Obvious of my surrounds
My mind in alert edgy state
Helpless eyes darted around
With a depleted heart
Supposedly natural things
A chore to my mind
I require some break
From habitual routine
To indulge in trance
To rekindle my urge
To live my life
At times I………

# हस्ती

कुछ बात है कि
हस्ती मिटती नहीं हमारी
गुज़रा हुआ साथ हमारा
रहेगा इस ज़माने में
सूरज की रोशनी सा खिलता हुआ
हवा के संग ठहरता हुआ
चाँद से प्यार करता हुआ
लहरों के संग बहता हुआ
हम नहीं तो क्या
हमारी हस्ती सदा रहेगी
कुछ तो बात है
हस्ती मिटती नहीं हमारी

Do you know
Who am I
I am complicated
With simple needs
I need to be alone
Need books to read
Old songs to listen
Dream with eyes wide open
Someone not to take care
But to care for me
Most importantly
To cherish and rekindle
My memories
Now say do you know
Who am I

# बवंडर

समुद्र के किनारे बैठी
पानी को ताकते हुए
ना जाने दिल कहाँ खो गया
पानी के बवंडर से
यादों के बवंडर तक
भुलाए न भूलें यादें
पानी के बवंडर से बचाएं
पर यादों के बवंडर से
बचना मुश्किल ही नहीं नामुमकिन
तोहफा है यह मिला हुआ
किसी एक को कैसे चुनें
एक दिल है तो दूसरा धड़कन
एक मुकद्दर तो दूसरी ज़रूरत
अपनी ओर खींचते हुए
निकलूँगी नहीं समा जाऊंगी
हमेशा के लिये इस बवंडर में

Loneliness
Been a part of me
Thought it will pass
With time, marriage
Children, age etc
but no it stayed put
my other half
it kind of fills
the void in life
I kinda enjoy it
Always with me
Like shadow
Merged into me
To become one
Me and my loneliness

# तू

तू इतनी खूबसूरत है

मुझे तेरी ज़रूरत है

तेरे बिना जीना नहीं

तेरे संग ही जीना है

तू मेरे दिल की धडकन

तू मेरी सांसें

तू मेरी खुशी

तू ही मेरा ग़म

तेरे संग ही जीना

तेरी बाँहों में मरना

तू ही मेरा जुनून

तू ही मेरी जिदंगी

तू इतनी........

Writing gives freedom
Freedom from sorrows
Freedom from pain
Freedom from wanting
Freedom from all traumas
It's a pacifying experience
It's a wonderful way of
Kidnapping our mind
Kidnapping of present
Mingling with past
Leaving a memory for future
It's what my writing is
Lasting long after I've gone
An everlasting gift
Of a special era

# तुम क्या हो...

मैं नहीं जानती तुम क्या हो
ज़िन्दगी हो, या सजा हो
अपना हो, या पराया
अमृत हो, या विष
अँधेरा हो, या उजाला
आशा हो, या निराशा
आंसू हो, या हँसी
दोस्त हो, या दुश्मन
नसीब हो, या बदनसीब
ज़िन्दगी हो, या मौत
पर जो भी हो
तुम मेरी ज़िन्दगी हो

It is night
Moonless and starless
Night high over the city
Over the dark flowing river
Night everywhere
With a forbidden frown
Of do not disturb looming high
At times stars peeping
Behind the clouds
Teasing the dark night
Silent message passing through
The dark forbidden night
Can't help blushing with lovely smile
After all the dark night and stars
Have been in love
Nobody knows for how long

# हम

अगर तुम खामोशी चाहो

तो मैं रात हूँ

अगर तुम कुछ कहना चाहो

तो मैं हमराज़ हूँ

अगर तुम कुछ देखना चाहो

तो मैं नज़ारा हूँ

अगर तुम डूबना चाहो

तो मैं समुंद्र हूँ

अगर तुम जीना चाहो

तो मैं सांसें हूँ

न तुम हो, न मैं हूँ

हम हमेशा हम हैं

I like myself on paper
Black and white
I find it very vivid

I thrive on paper
My dreams endure in paper
And remain alive forever

Conjure up life
The way I want
Stress free Tension free
Commitment-nil

Full of love & laughter
Pampering me
Cherishing me for life
I like myself on paper

# ख़्वाहिशें

किसी से कहना चाहूँ
तो किससे कहूँ
लाखों ख़्वाहिशें हैं दिल में
नहीं एक भी जुबान पर
क्या कभी कह पाओगी
अपनी ख़्वाहिशेंकिसी से
या वो भी दफन हो जायेंगी
मेरे सपनों की तरह मेरे साथ
अधूरी यह ख़्वाहिशें......

You will want to talk
Want to laugh with me
Want to yell at me
Have quixotic talk with me
Want to hug me
Want to look at me
One day you will miss me
I will be too far
You will have to do
With my memories
As I can't see tears
In your eyes
Alive or dead

# याद

तुझे देखने के लिये

न आँखों की ज़रूरत है

न कोई तस्वीर की

तुझे याद करने के लिये

न वज़ह की ज़रूरत है

न कोई बहाने की

तुझे सुनने के लिये

न तेरी ज़रूरत है

न तेरी आवाज़ की

पर एक दिन तेरी ज़रूरत है

इस आखिरी खूबसूरत मुलाकात में

मै रहूँ या न रहूँ

मेरी जान रहेगी तेरे पास

तेरी याद रहेगी मेरे दिल में

The little droplets
Standard in the brim of eyes
Trying hard to stay in
Also wanting to come out

These pearl drops
Not a sign of weakness
But a sign of love

Feelings beyond
Heart and minds comprehension
Flows out of eyes
Like a droplets of pearl

A tiny smile on lips
Accompanying pearl drops
Creak volumes without words

I would like to hold
Till my end
But alas, can't deprive
The heart's desire
To speak without words

# ना जाने क्या देखा

ना जाने क्या देखा
उसने मेरी निगाह में
उसके होठों पर
एक मीठी सी मुस्कान आयी
और चेहरा खिल उठा
कुछ तो है मेरी निगाहों में
जो उसकी निगाहें देख सकी
जो उसको बहुत पसंद है
जो लब्ज़ मुकम्मल नहीं कर पाए
उसे निगाहें कर गई
हम पे ऐतबार कर गई
दिल पे एहसान कर गई
ना जाने क्या देखा........

Life is just a pinprick
Just bear it
You can't have a life
Happy, happier and happiest
It's a mixture of all
Just experience it
When happy enjoy life
When sad cry like a hurricane
Just experience it
Real flowers few, dead many
The fragrance of dead flower
Helps to cross the hurricane
Don't discard them carry them
Life is a pinprick
Just experience it

# चाँद

चाँद मुस्कराये

जब हवा कुछ कहे

जैसे कोई ख़ास

कुछ कह रहा हो

चांदनी को ले चलो

उसके चाँद के पास

दूरियों का ग़म नहीं

फासलों का एहसास नहीं

जब बसेरा दिल में है

क्या दूरियाँ क्या फासले

हवा में बातों का नशा

दिल में चाँद का नशा

लिये अपने संग चले

मुस्कुराती हुई चांदनी

चाँद........

The sun and the moon
Were very much in love
But cannot stay together
The sun needed light and
The moon darkness to live
The sun died day after day to
Allow his moon to breath
the moon died for sun to shine
They desired to meet
Hence they came together
Once in a while
They rejoice on seeing each other
For that special moment
They wait every single day of life

# आगोश

यादों के आगोश में
हकीकत की आड़ में
गुज़रती हई ज़िन्दगी
कभी हाथों से फिसले
पानी की तरह
तो कभी अटल रहे
लकीरों की तरह
फिसलती अटल ज़िन्दगी
का एक ही सहारा
आगोश यादों का

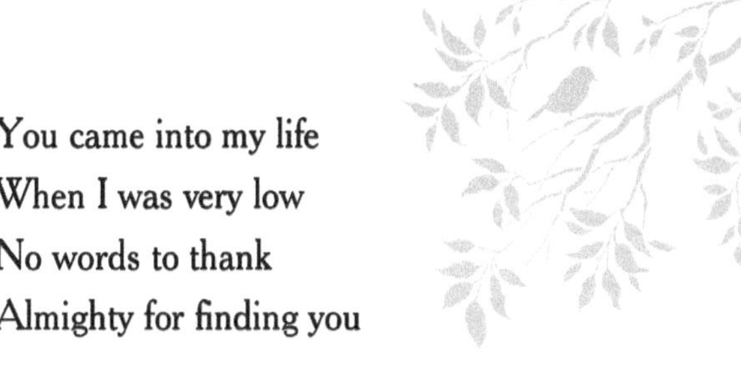

You came into my life
When I was very low
No words to thank
Almighty for finding you

You stood by my side
Sacrificing your career
For keeping me alive
But for your sacrifice
I would be a photo
On the wall

I want you by my side
Holding my hand
Guiding me in my life

I want to leave this world
With my loved ones
And you by my side
Holding my hand

# इंतज़ार है

तुझसे मिलने का
बातें करने का
दीदार करने का
सेवा करने का
सुनने का
मुझे इंतज़ार है
बातें सुनने का
दर्शन देने का
सेवा करवाने का
मुझे इंतज़ार है

My buddy
Four decades old
Feels incredibly new
Like a ray of hope
In the channel of darkness
Filling the void
Fastening the belt of
Togetherness of love
We landed in our life
Thanks for tolerating
Me and my idiocy
It s a privilege
having a buddy like you

# देखा है हमने

देखा है हमने
बिछुड़ते हुए
किस्मत को
रुठते हुए
ज़िन्दगी को
बहते हुए
आँसुओं को
ठहरते हुए
ख़्वाबों को
पर खूबसूरत है
ज़िन्दगी
ज़िन्दगी का सफर
यूँ ही काटते चलें

I don't know what to say
When you looked into my eyes
All my dreams came true
On seeing the love in your face
The light in your eyes
The smile for which I could die
My heart skipped a beat
Wish I could close my eyes
With the feeling of fulfilled love
Once and for all
Seeing you one last time
With the love and smile
The beginning of journey
To eternal with peaceful soul

# कुछ करना नहीं पड़ा

कुछ करना नहीं पड़ा
कोई मंजिल नहीं
रास्ता ढूँढना नहीं पड़ा
कोई मिलने वाला नहीं
घर से निकलना नहीं पड़ा
कोई सुनने वाला नहीं
बातें करना नहीं पड़ा
कोई सपना नहीं
जीना नहीं पड़ा
मन में कोई आशा नहीं
मन्दिर जाना नहीं पड़ा
खुदा ने मुझे ज़िन्दगी दी
जो मैंने आज़माया ज़िन्दगीको
मगर कुछ करना नहीं पड़ा

U before I
Its always U before I
Ur well being before mine
Ur happiness before mine
Ur smile before mine
Ur more vital then I
I will do anything for U
I can never be prior to U
I will always be prior to U
In all bad deeds of life
For rest of everything
Child like guileless
Its my heartfelt craving
U before I

# ख़्वाहिश

जीने की ख़्वाहिश में

ख़्वाबों से दोस्ती कर बैठे

ख़्वाबों से ज़्यादा

आँसुओं से दोस्ती कर बैठे

आंसुओं से ज़्यादा

तन्हाई से दोस्ती कर बैठे

तन्हाई से ज़्यादा

तुमसे दोस्ती कर बैठे

तुमसे ज़्यादा

खामोशी से दोस्ती कर बैठे

क्योंकि तन्हाई और खामोशी के सिवाय

कोई अपना होता ही नहीं

Come spend a day with me
I know I am not perfect
I am a big crazy, moody
With varied choice
You have better friends
Beautiful and intelligent
I am just ordinary
These are no issues
Spend a crazy day
Only me for company
You might miss
The most beautiful
And memorable
Day of your life
Come spend a day with me

# आशा

नींद आती नहीं

पर नींद में रहती हूँ

ख़्वाब देखती नहीं

पर ख़्वाब में चलती हूँ

हँसी आती नहीं

पर हँसती रहती हूँ

ज़िन्दगी जीती नहीं

पर ज़िन्दा रहती हूँ

ख़ुदा से कोई चाह नहीं

पर मन में आशा भरे रहती हूँ

At work
I'm busy
I don't have time
Its that simple
At home
I'm busy
I don't have time
Its that simple
Work or home
I'm always busy
I don't have time
Its that simple
Life is so simple
What is complicated
Its me I am complicated
I don't understand
The simplicity of life
It's that simple

# तन्हाई

एक मुख़्तसर अल्फ़ाज़
जो नूर की तरह है
जिसका ख़ौफ सब को है
जिसकी ताबीर मुश्किल है
मेरी इबादत है
न कोई ख़ौफ है या डर
सिर्फ एक जज़्बा
एक राब्ता जैसी
रूहानियत है मेरी
जुस्तजू न होए कम
एक मुख़्तसर अल्फ़ाज़
मैं और मेरी तन्हाई
ज़िन्दगी है

Beauty known to few
Your eye shines bright
Like the rays of sun
The expressions so immense
Draws like a magnet
Keeps me glad
Alas, beauty known to few
Your lovely beautiful smile
Like oasis in desert
Like dew drops on petals
Lighten up your whole face
Like sun shining through snow
I can't get you out of sight
But, Alas, beauty known to few

# इरादा

ज़िन्दगी में सब बदल जाता है
राह चलते-चलते
रास्ते बदल जाते हैं
वक्त की आंधी में
सब कुछ खो जाता है
इंसान बदल जाते हैं
जाने कब तूफ़ान आता है
हमें हमारी मंजिल से
दूर उड़ा ले जाता है
जब तक हम संभलते हैं
सब कुछ खो जाता है
सोचती हूँ तुझे इतना याद न करूँ
सवेरा होते ही इरादा बदल जाता है

Life is full of ups and downs
Living behind memories
Some old and some new
Placing a tangible hold
Perpetually on our heart
Handful of memories
Galloping towards us
Along with mouthful of love
Like a nectar
living in and around us
Life is full of memories
Handful and Mouthful

# चाहत

नज़र चाहती है
दीदार करना
कान चाहतेहैं
आवाज़ सुनना
दिल चाहता है
तेरे पास खामोश रहना
हाथ चाहते हैं
तेरा हाथ थामना
ज़िन्दगी चाहती है
तुझे अपने पास रखना
नसीब में लिखा है
यादों में खुश रहना

That's the thing about pain
It demands to be felt
That the thing about tears
It insist on flowing out
That's the thing about smile
It demands to be articulated
That's the thing about dreams
It has to be twisted and wrecked
That's the thing about life
It demands to be infinite

# मोहब्बत

ख़ामोशी से कहने वाली
दिल के अल्फ़ाज़
जो कोई सुन नहीं सकता
जीने का सहारा है
खूबसूरत है वो लम्हा
जब कोई दिल में बसता है
वो मिले या ना मिले
ख्वाबों के सहारे
ज़िन्दगी गुज़र जाती है
निस्वार्थ मोहब्बत करना
अपने आप में खास है
आजकल किसी को याद
बिना मतलब के कौन करता है

Things are not what all sees
It is not sheer tears that flows
It is unfulfilled desire
It is not killer smile all sees
It is colossal pain
It is not mere memories
It is the soul of existence
It is not just words which flows
It is emotions indescribable
It is not just poems
It is lost life gasping for breath
It is all what you see
It is all how you see
It is a kind of message
It is how you interpret
As things are not what all sees

Things I can never control
My smile when I see you
My tears when I miss you
My fears when I think of you
My delight when I see you succeed
My prayers for your wellness
When everything is for you
What is for me
It's just me and you
Always have and always will

I am not absent minded
It is the presence of mind
That makes me unaware of things
I am not a dreamer
It is the presence of dream
That makes life livable
I am not a poet
It is the presence of memories
That makes me write poems
I am not somebody
It is the presence of you
That makes me somebody

I would like to be
Unnoticed but necessary
I would like to be the air
That you breathe in
Unnoticed but necessary
I would like to be the light
That emblazes your life
Unnoticed but necessary
I would like to be the water
That quenches your thirst
Unnoticed but necessary
I would like to be your heart beat
That keeps you going
Unnoticed but necessary
I would like to be
In your life
Unnoticed but necessary

The moon
My inimitable ally
It lightens the whole world
It is special for me
It shines for me to smile
Winks to brighten me up
Glazing at me with love
Makes me feel cherished
It never beams
Without bringing me dreams
The never diminishing bond
Between me and my moon

The abode of love
Is not illuminated
By material things
It is illuminated
By happiness
In the core of heart
It is scarce opulence
Experienced
In densest darkness
Unbounded by virtue
Of any materialist illusions
To be cherished lifelong
The adobe of love

When I look through my life
I find doom and gloom
I look through my dull life
And go into the world of dreams
I do and see things I like
I see a dew drop on petal
Cling ling to life
a teardrops out of my eyes
A smile settles on my lips
For a second I forget my pain
I stop breathing for a while
Suddenly awake gulping for air
The world of dreams falls apart
The wounded heart aches
The pain unbearable
The soul resorts to silence
And looks through my life

# जान

थोड़ा और रुको न
आई हो इतनी दूर से
मुझसे मिलने
थोड़ा और रुको न
बातें हैं ढेर सारी
कुछ कहना है
कुछ सुनना है
दिल में उमड़ती हुई
यह ख़्वाहिशें
कुछ पूरी तो कुछ अधूरी
तरसती हुई निगाहों को
थोड़ा दीदार करने दो
तड़पते हुए दिल को
थोड़ा चैन पाने दो
ओय जान थोड़ा और रूको ना

www.ingramcontent.com/pod-product-compliance
Lightning Source LLC
LaVergne TN
LVHW041756190726
843493LV00008B/2656